SKATEBOARDING HIST

Skateboarding was invented in the 1930s. Kids w̶h̶o̶ with rollerskates experimented by attaching them to a wooden board. The objective was to start at the top of a hill and ride down. Seemed simple, but just staying on the board and not crashing took some doing! "Sidewalk surfing", as it was known then, really took off in 1958 when a surf shop teamed up with a rollerskate manufacturer to produce the first commercial wheeled skateboards.

Now, thanks to improvements in equipment design and materials, and with superstars like Tony Hawk performing all over the world, skateboarding is definitely here to stay!

SKATELIST

street skating: skating on roads, curbs, handrails and other elements of urban landscapes

vert skating: skating on ramps and other vertical structures specifically designed for skating

half pipe: a u-shaped ramp of any size, usually with a flat section in the middle

vert ramp: a half-pipe, usually at least 8 feet (2.5 meters) tall, with steep sides that are vertical near the top

goofy: riding with the right foot forward, the opposite of "regular"

regular: riding with the left foot forward, the opposite of "goofy"

switch stance: riding the board with the opposite footing from usual, i.e., "goofy" instead of "regular"

kickstart

BOARD>ESSENTIALS ·

first stuff

GET TO KNOW YOUR BOARD

If you want to get into skateboarding it's a good idea to know a little about your board. Skateboards can be expensive – but because your first board will probably take a bit of a battering why not pick up a hard-wearing cheap model or even a secondhand board? It's important to get yourself some padding for your knees and elbows and a helmet to protect your head. When you've mastered the basics you might consider buying a lightweight board that will help you pull off more tricks.

DECK: the flat standing surface of a skateboard, usually laminated maple

GRIP TAPE: sandpaper fixed to the top of the deck with adhesive, used to increase the friction between the deck and the skater's feet

NOSE: from the front of the skateboard to the front truck bolts

RAIL: the edge of the skateboard and if fitted, plastic strips attached to the board's underside

TAIL: the rear of the skateboard, from the back truck bolts to the end

TRUCKS: the front and rear axle assemblies that connect the wheels to the deck and provide the turning capabilities for the board

WHEELS: usually made of polyurethane and sized between 3.9 and 6.6 centemeters in diameter; their hardness is measured by a durometer, a number ranging from 0 to 100. Soft wheels have a durometer of about 85, hard wheels have a durometer of 97 or higher

WHEELBASE: the distance between the front and back wheels, measured between the two sets of innermost truck holes

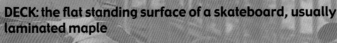

BOARD MANIA

BASIC STANCE

The basic stance on a skateboard is your choice; some people are "regular" and some "goofy". Regular stance is when you ride left foot to the front and right foot to the back. Goofy is the exact opposite – right foot leading and left foot to the back. Just decide which one feels most comfortable for you. Next put your lead foot right over the front screws, parallel with the board, then with your back foot, push off and then switch your feet onto the board so that your front foot turns 90° sideways and your back foot is similarly sideways on the tail. That is the basic stance of skateboarding.

BOARD MAINTENANCE

Replacing the grip tape on your board is often overlooked, but can make a big difference to the quality of tricks you can land.

Wheels, trucks, bearings and deck can also be changed, interchanged and upgraded as you gain confidence and experience.

NOW GET ON YOUR BOARD!

DANGER

Will you become a top trix skater?

MISSION
XTREME
3D

MISSION · XTREME

trick list

AIR: all four wheels off the ground

BACKSIDE: when a trick is executed with the skater's back facing the ramp or obstacle

CARVE: skating in a long, curving arc

FAKIE: skating backwards – the skater is standing in his or her normal stance, but the board is moving backwards

FRONTSIDE: when a trick is executed with the front of the skater's body facing the ramp or obstacle

GRIND: scraping one or both axles on a curb, railing or other surface

KICKFLIP: a variation on the ollie – the skater kicks the board into a spin before landing back on it

MONGO-FOOT: a style of pushing where the back foot is kept on the board and pushing is done with the front foot

NOLLIE: an ollie performed by tapping the nose of the board instead of the tail

NOSESLIDE: sliding the underside of the nose end of a board on a ledge or lip

OLLIE: a jump made by tapping the tail of the board on the ground; the basis of most skating tricks

RAILSLIDE: a trick in which the skater slides the underside of the deck along an object, such as a curb or handrail

SHOVE-IT: spinning the board 180° beneath the feet while travelling forward

TAILSLIDE: sliding the underside of the tail end of a board on a ledge or lip

STOP
motion

OLLIE
Frame-by-frame
xtreme ollie

Take off
Hang
Don't lose it
Landed!
How high?
How long?
You'd never believe it!

BOARD MANIA

frontside ollie

TRICK or treat

GRIND

Find a rail or other long edge. Jump, balance and distance – that's what makes a great grind!

BOARD DEBRIEF

Question 1
When was skateboarding invented?
A: 19th Century B: Early 1900s C: 1980s

WOW! nose grind in 3D!

DANGER

MISSION XTREME 3D

MISSION · XTREME

ollie up

THE FIRST TRICK every skater should learn is the ollie. Invented by Alan "Ollie" Gelfand, it is the technique a skater uses to jump over, on to or up to an obstacle. All the time the board appears to stick to the skater's feet. It's the basic skateboarding trick from which many other tricks follow. But landing an ollie isn't easy and it will take hours of practice to perfect!

STEP ONE
Place your back foot on the tail (back) of the board. Put your front foot halfway between the nose (front) and the tail.

STEP TWO
Get ready to make the jump by crouching down – this lowers your center of gravity. Push down on the tail of the board with your back foot.

STEP THREE
Now straighten your legs – jumping in the air. The downward force on the tail will make the board bounce upwards.

STEP FOUR
As the board rises, drag your front foot forward to the nose. Then push down on the nose of the board with your front foot.

STEP FIVE
Lift your rear foot, allowing the tail to rise as downward force is applied to the nose. The jump reaches its peak and the board should be level. Gravity will now take hold. As you land, absorb the impact by once more bending your legs.

LANDED!

stop motion

NOLLIE
Frame-by-frame xtreme nollie

You must first feel confident with your ollies to perform this trick, as it is an ollie off the nose while going forward, a n(ose) ollie or nollie!

BOARD DEBRIEF

Question 2
What type of wood are most skateboards made of?
 A: Pine   B: Maple   C: Oak

switchstance ollie

BOARD MANIA

BACKSIDE OLLIE · · · ·
Take off – landing 180°

TRICK or treat

6

7

8

DANGER

Frontside boardslide

MISSION 3D

MISSION · XTREME

streetsupreme

STOP motion

FRONTSIDE AIR
Frame-by-frame
xtreme frontside air

THE STREET – The real heart of skateboarding where we look for the radical spirit and freedom of true boarding. At one with your board, adapting to your environment, using the hard urban landscape, molding it, feeling it, freeing it. Pure.

BOARD DEBRIEF

Question 3
What was skateboarding originally called?
A: Streetboarding B: Curb cruising C: Sidewalk surfing

BOARD MANIA

heelflip

360 KICKFLIP
This one's tricky!
Flipping your board 360° mid-jump

TRICK or treat

4

5

6

DANGER

Frontside boardslide

MISSION XTREME 3D

MISSION.XTREME.

slide
slide

Grinds

Scraping one or both axles on a curb, railing or other surface such as:

CROOKED GRIND – grinding on only the front truck while sliding
50-50 GRIND – grinding on both trucks equally
NOSEGRIND – grinding on only the front truck
5-0 GRIND – grinding on only the back truck

CROOKED
Frame-by-frame
xtreme crooked

STOP motion

noseslide

BOARD MANIA

12

NOSEGRIND • • • • • • • • • • •
Grind on only the front truck

TRICK or treat

6

7

8

Xtreme 360° flip

BOARD DEBRIEF

Question 4
Which of the following is NOT a skateboarding trick?
A: Ollie   B: Tail Grind   C: Funky chicken flip

XTREME MISSION 3D

BOARD>TRIX>5.

Vert ramp trix

Xtreme skateboarding trix performed on a half-pipe, usually at least 8 feet (2.5 meters) tall, with steep sides that are perfectly vertical near the top.

Tony Hawk, pictured here executing a huge frontside air, is one of the world's greatest supporters of vert boarding.

**LIPSLIDE
Frame-by-frame
xtreme lipslide**

liftoff

STOP. motion

BOARD DEBRIEF

Question 5
Which character in "The Simpsons" loves to skateboard?
A: Bart Simpson B: Homer Simpson C: Monty Burns

backside tailslide

BOARD MANIA

HUGE 50-50 • • • • • • • • • • • •
**Speed grind at the
Euro Championship**

TRICK or **treat**

5

6

7

DANGER

Half-pipe trix take a great deal of practice

MISSION XTREME **3D**

(15)

STOP. motion
board heroes

The world's best skateboarders have become sporting heroes recognized the world over. Developing and performing sometimes totally outrageous stunts and tricks, these guys look to push boarding to the absolute extreme! Pro-boarders often sign up deals to ride for specific manufacturers – using their boards and facilities when taking part in competitions all around the world. Probably the most famous pro-skateboarders are Tony Hawk and Steve Berra.

BACKSIDE AIR
Frame-by-frame
xtreme backside air

BOARD MANIA

kickflip

16

Question 6
Who invented the ollie?
A: Tony Hawk B: Alan Gelfand C: Zachary Taylor

TAIL GRIND · · · · · · · · · ·
balance and control

TRICK or treat

5

6

7

DANGER

Tony Hawk in mid-flight in this xtreme half pipe maneuver

XTREME MISSION 3D

MISSION · XTREME

megatrix

STOP motion

ROCK TO FAKIE
Frame-by-frame
xtreme rock to fakie

Steve Berra –
professional skateboarder

Steve was really into bikes until he moved to Nebraska when he was 13. Every kid there was into skateboarding. Steve got a skateboard on his birthday and hasn't stopped since! When he was 15 he realized he was better than all the people who used to be the best: "I was like wow! I'm lucky the only thing I had to do in Nebraska was skate!" Steve prefers street skating to half-pipes and ramps. No pain, no gain!

frontside
tailslide

18